Life in World War II

Brian Williams

www.raintreepublishers.co.uk
Visit our website to find out more information about Raintree books.

To order:
☎ Phone 0845 6044371
📠 Fax +44 (0) 1865 312263
💻 Email myorders@raintreepublishers.co.uk

Customers from outside the UK please telephone +44 1865 312262

Raintree is an imprint of Capstone Global Library Limited, a company incorporated in England and Wales having its registered office at 7 Pilgrim Street, London, EC4V 6LB - Registered company number: 6695582

Edited by Kate de Villiers and Laura Knowles
Designed by Steve Mead and Debbie Oatley
Original illustrations © Capstone Global Library Limited 2010
Illustrations by Jeff Edwards
Picture research by Mica Brancic and Elaine Willis
Production by Alison Parsons
Originated by Chroma Graphics (Overseas) Pte. Ltd
Printed and bound in China by Leo Paper Products Ltd

ISBN 978 0 431193 62 5 (hardback)
14 13 12 11 10
10 9 8 7 6 5 4 3 2 1

ISBN 978 0 431193 69 4 (paperback)
15 14 13 12 11 10
10 9 8 7 6 5 4 3 2

British Library Cataloguing in Publication Data
Williams, Brian, 1943-
Life in World War II. -- (Unlocking history)
941'.084-dc22
A full catalogue record for this book is available from the British Library.

Acknowledgements
We would like to thank the following for permission to reproduce photographs: We would like to thank the following for permission to reproduce photographs: Alamy p. **19** (© Lordprice Collection Corbis); p. **17** (© Hulton-Deutsch Collection); Getty Images pp. **5** (New York Times Co.), **7** (Fox Photos), **8** (Fox Photos), **10** (Hulton Archive/Fox Photos), **13** (Central Press), **15** (Keystone), **18** (Popperfoto), **20** (Hulton Archive), **23** (Fox Photos/A. J. O'Brien), **25** (Hulton Archive/Fox Photos), **26** (Hulton Archive/FPG), **27** (Fox Photos/William Vanderson), **28** (Fox Photos); TopFoto p. **22**.

Cover photograph of evacuee children in 1941 reproduced with permission of Corbis/© Hulton-Deutsch Collection.

We would like to thank Bill Marriott for his invaluable help in the preparation of this book.

Every effort has been made to contact copyright holders of material reproduced in this book. Any omissions will be rectified in subsequent printings if notice is given to the publishers.

All the Internet addresses (URLs) given in this book were valid at the time of going to press. However, due to the dynamic nature of the Internet, some addresses may have changed, or sites may have changed or ceased to exist since publication. While the author and Publishers regret any inconvenience this may cause readers, no responsibility for any such changes can be accepted by either the author or the Publishers.

Contents

Some words are shown in **bold**, like this. You can find out what they mean by looking in the glossary.

World war

A war is when countries fight one another. In the 20th century there were two "world wars" in which many countries took part. In World War I (1914–18) about 21 million people were killed. World War II (1939–45) lasted longer and even more people were killed – between 35 and 60 million. No one knows the exact number because records were often not kept, some were lost, and many dead bodies were never found.

World War II was fought mainly in Europe, Africa, and Asia. In Europe, it began when Germany attacked Poland. Britain and France then went to war with Germany. Canada, Australia, and other countries from the Commonwealth joined Britain. The Commonwealth includes countries that used to be part of the British Empire. Italy, Hungary, and Romania took Germany's side. By 1941, USSR (Russia), Japan, and the United States were in the war, too. In the end, the **Allies** (Britain, France, United States, USSR, and other nations) defeated the **Axis Powers** (Germany, Italy, Japan, and others).

▼ This map shows the main areas of fighting: Europe, USSR, North Africa and the Mediterranean Sea, and the Pacific Ocean.

Maps show how World War II was fought in many places across the world.

The war had a big impact on children. Many were killed in fighting or **air raids**. Many more died of hunger and disease. Millions of families lost their homes.

We know about World War II from **evidence**, such as books, photographs, films, radio broadcasts, posters, diaries, and people's memories. This book explains how different kinds of evidence can unlock history, to show us what life was like for people at war.

▼ This family practised wearing **gas masks** in May 1939, four months before the war began.

Britain at war

War did not come as a surprise in 1939. People had read in books and newspapers about Germany's **Nazi** leader, Adolf Hitler. He wanted Germany to control a new empire in Europe. People had watched **newsreels** of fighting in Spain, China, and Abyssinia (Ethiopia). Some German Jews (people who follow the religion of Judaism) fled to Britain as refugees. Refugees are people fleeing from their own country in search of safety, usually from fighting or a disaster of some kind. The Jews told stories of violence, imprisonment, and murder by the Nazis.

In 1938, every British family was given **gas masks**, or "respirators". These were breathing kits, to wear if enemy planes dropped poison-gas bombs. By the summer of 1939, mothers had been told to take their children out of the cities, in case there were **air raids**. The **evacuation** plans told everyone that war was likely.

Air force sizes in 1939

	Type of aeroplane	
	Bombers	Fighters
Germany	1,050	1,000
Britain	536	608
France	463	634

Britain and France together had more aeroplanes than Germany, but many were out of date. This table does not show how many of the planes were modern.

On 1 September 1939, German armies and planes attacked Poland. Britain and France were **allies** of Poland, and had agreed to help Poland. But Hitler refused to stop. On 3rd September came the news on the radio and in newspaper headlines: "WAR!" Soldiers, sailors, and airmen said goodbye to their families. Warships were put to sea. Planes stood ready on airfields. At home, people waited to see what would happen next.

▲ Soldiers read the war news on 3 September 1939. Do you think they really felt as cheerful as they look?

Evacuation

The government feared that bombing from the air would cause panic. It made **evacuation** plans to move 3 million children and mothers away from cities that would be targets for enemy planes.

In August 1939, before the war began, thousands of children had already left home. They crowded onto trains. Each child wore a name tag, and carried a bag with clothes, books, comics, sandwiches, and a **gas mask** in a cardboard box. Going off in a train was quite exciting, but most children were sad to leave their homes, toys, pets, and parents. They were now known as **evacuees**.

▼ This photo was taken on 1st September 1939. It shows children being evacuated on buses to take them out of London.

This pie chart shows the different groups of people that were evacuated from towns and cities during the first planned evacuation in 1939, called "Operation Pied Piper". A total of around 1.5 million people were evacuated. Most of these were children.

A pie chart helps us compare the sizes of different groups.

12,000 pregnant women

7,000 people with disabilities

100,000 teachers and helpers

500,000 mothers and young children

800,000 children

Evacuees went to stay with host-families, who were paid just under £1 a week for two children. By 1941 the payment was cut to 8s 6d (about 47p) for a child under 10, and 15s (75p) for teenagers. Some hosts were like new aunts and uncles, and made a fuss of the new arrivals. Others grumbled that city children were rude, dirty, and ate too much!

The value of money

Until 1971, British money was in pounds, shillings, and pence (written as £1 1s 1d). There were 20 shillings in a pound. One pound was worth a lot more than it is now. It is not easy to compare prices with today's.

At first, there was not much bombing, and by January 1940 more than 900,000 children had come home. Some people said the war would soon be over. Others waited to see when the fighting would really start.

Evacuees were given postcards to write and post home. In April 1941, a schoolgirl evacuee wrote to her father: "... I have made a bet with Anne Parker that the war will be over by the end of September. If it isn't I have to give her a bar of chocolate (if I can get it), if it is she has to give me one."

Letters from child evacuees help to show us how they felt and what they hoped might happen.

Everyone's war

The war brought everyone new experiences. Some **evacuees** had their first car ride, from a country station to their wartime home, or "billet". Many had never been away from home before. Country cottage toilets could be scary – a shed in the garden, very dark, and full of spiders!

A teacher told his class that rabbits were a bit like cats (none of the town children had seen a wild rabbit before). Next day there was rabbit pie for school dinner, but no one would eat it. Town children also had their first sight of farm animals. One wrote about a cow: "At the back it has a tail on which hangs a brush. With this it sends the flies away so that they do not fall into the milk."

▼ This photograph, taken in June 1940, shows evacuees enjoying an outdoor maths lesson in Wales.

Photos like this were published to show people how evacuee children were enjoying country life – and learning, too.

Winston Churchill

In May 1940, Winston Churchill (1874–1965) became Britain's prime minister. He used radio to speak to the nation, and his stirring words raised people's spirits. When Britain faced invasion in 1940, Churchill said: "we shall fight in the fields and in the streets ... we shall never surrender".

Adults also learned lots of new things. The war mixed people from different parts of Britain, and from other countries. Rich and poor, men and women, old and young, all worked side by side. Everyone had to queue at shops, and squeeze onto crowded buses and trains. Most people knew someone who was away fighting.

From 1940, people across Britain faced real danger. First there was the threat of a German **invasion**, then attack from the skies in the **Blitz**.

Some good and bad things about being an evacuee

Some things the government thought would be good for evacuees:	Some things evacuees complained about:
Meeting new people	Missing my friends
Fewer shops, less traffic	Too quiet, can't sleep
No films	Bored, nothing to do
Going to bed early	Missing mum and my own bed
Fresh vegetables to eat	No fish and chip shops
Fresh air and exercise	Missing street games

The Blitz on Britain

In the summer of 1940, the German air force or Luftwaffe began raids on Britain. Fighter planes of the Royal Air Force fought off the attacks, winning what became known as the Battle of Britain. "We used to sit on a gate and watch the planes," one **evacuee** remembered. "Once a German plane flew very close, but the pilot just waved."

That summer, people got ready for a German **invasion**. It never came. Instead, German planes began bombing London and other cities. This was the **Blitz**. On 7 September 1940, more than 300 people were killed in an **air raid** on London. On 14 November, German planes bombed Coventry. Other cities were bombed, including Birmingham, Manchester, Glasgow, Belfast, Swansea, Liverpool, and Hull.

Children got used to air raids – the wailing sound of devices called sirens before the planes came overhead, and then the "all clear" siren when the raid was over. They saw fires in the street and heard the thump of exploding bombs and houses collapsing. They slept in **shelters**. Thousands of Londoners spent the nights in Underground stations, sleeping on the platforms.

This photograph, of people in Canterbury after an air raid, was taken in 1942. The 1940 Blitz was only the start of the bombing of Britain's towns.

Beating the invader

A government leaflet called *Beating the Invader* told people
what to do if German soldiers landed in Britain in 1940:

- Stay where you are (don't travel)
- Carry on going to work and school
- Listen for church bells (a warning of parachute landings)
- Listen to the wireless (the radio) for news
- If you have a car, put it out of action and burn any maps
- Do not help the enemy in any way.

Government documents show us
what information people were given
during wartime. Why do you think
people were told not to travel?

Taking shelter

Air raids meant sleepless nights. Enemy planes usually flew over at night. When sirens sounded the air raid warning, people hurried into **shelters**. Thousands of homes had an Anderson shelter in the garden. The indoor Morrison shelter was a metal cage, big enough to sleep inside.

A high-explosive bomb could wreck a house. Fire-bombs started fires. For defence, Britain had fighter planes and anti-aircraft guns to shoot down enemy planes, and **civil defence** workers. Civil defence workers included firefighters, police, ARP (Air Raid Precautions) wardens, first-aid teams, and rescuers who dug out people buried beneath bombed buildings. Other people mended electricity wires and gas pipes, filled holes in roads, and repaired damaged buildings. The post and milk were still delivered, even in streets littered with rubble from bombed buildings.

Every raid left people homeless. In Liverpool, 40,000 people needed re-housing in just one week in May 1941. By the end of 1941, over 200,000 bombs had hit London and 500,000 people had lost their homes. In 1944, people in southern England faced attacks from German V-1 "flying bombs" and V-2 rockets.

Memories

Audrey Bowen, aged 13, remembered taking rugs into their shelter, to keep warm. She and her mum wore trousers for the first time, too. Her pet tortoise and cat came into the shelter as well.

People's memories can be useful historical evidence.

Instructions

These instructions come from a 1939 Ministry of Home Security poster. It told people what to do if the enemy dropped poison gas.

- If indoors, hold breath, put on **gas mask**, and close windows.
- If outdoors, put on gas mask and turn up coat collar.
- Put on gloves or keep hands in pockets.
- Take cover in the nearest building.

▼ This family has put up their Anderson shelter and has begun planting vegetables to grow over it.

Why were people told to close windows? Why put on gloves? How do you think people felt when they read these instructions?

Schools at war

Schools stayed open, though some were hit by bombs or moved into new buildings, away from the cities. Children practised **air raid** drills, a bit like school fire drills today. There were **casualties**. In 1943, a school in Catford, London, was bombed and thirty-eight children and six teachers were killed.

At school, children followed the war, sticking little flags on wall-maps to show battles. They pasted articles and photos from newspapers in scrapbooks. Outside of school, city children played on the ruins of buildings that had been hit by bombs. Children also hunted the streets and fields for small bits of bomb-metal or shot-down aircraft, to keep as souvenirs.

Some children saw soldiers training, such as Commandos in the Scottish mountains, or they met enemy prisoners of war who had been sent to work on farms. Children collected scrap metal for **recycling** to make warplanes. They bought savings stamps, as part of the National Savings scheme to help the war effort.

In class, children learned the same sort of things as they do today. Most young people left school at 14, to go to work. At 18, many could expect call-up. This was the government order to join the army, navy, or air force, or to do war work in a coal mine or factory.

Wartime toilets

Many schools took over old buildings with no toilet except an outdoor privy, which was often just a bucket. Senior pupils stood outside when it was the teacher's turn to use it.

Shelter kit

Which things would have been most useful in an air raid **shelter**?

- bottle of drink
- fishing net
- warm blanket
- playing cards
- comic
- torch
- bicycle
- football

Fun fact

One boy **evacuee** slept in a school hall. He used a large bun he'd been given as a pillow. In the morning, he ate his "pillow" for breakfast.

▼ People took shelter in the London Underground. They slept on the platform.

BOUNDS GREEN

Shelters were often cold, and a night could seem like a very long time!

Family life

The war was tough on families. Many fathers, and older brothers and sisters, were away from home for months or even years. While many fathers were in the **armed forces**, many mothers were out at work in offices and factories. **Air raids** meant sleepless nights, so everyone felt tired. Shopping often took hours, because there were long queues. Many foods, clothes, shoes, and other goods were **rationed**.

▲ This photograph from 1940 shows a family listening to news about the war on their radio.

Sometimes damage to water pipes meant there was no water from the taps. So as not to waste water, bath water was rationed to 13 centimetres (5 inches) of water once a week. Since most homes had coal fires, people shivered if they ran out of coal. Most homes had electric lights, though some still had old-fashioned gas lamps. If the electricity and gas were cut off, people lit candles.

At night, streets were dark because of the **blackout**. At home, children helped draw curtains over windows, to stop lights showing. Lights from houses and streets could guide enemy aircraft high overhead. With no street lights, it was easy to bump into things on a dark night, and there were more road accidents. People used small torches to help find their way around.

Christmas in the Blitz

Betty Westwell and her brother lived near Manchester. In 1940, they went Christmas shopping, and although air raids had smashed shop windows and scattered goods all over the street, Betty remembered:

"the Christmas decorations and trees were there, so everything seemed all right".

The next day, the Westwell family had a cold Christmas dinner by candlelight (bombs had cut off the gas and electricity). They ate tinned chicken, ham, fruit, and cold Christmas pudding.

Personal memories help bring history to life.

This is a clothing ration book from 1944. People were not allowed to buy clothes or food without their ration books.

1944-45 GENERAL CB1/7

CLOTHING BOOK

This book must not be used until the holder's name and full postal address have been written below.

HOLDER'S NAME _COURT, SARAH. J._ (in BLOCK letters)

ADDRESS _LUNGE CLIF RD. S.E.13._ (in BLOCK letters) _LEWISHAM_

Detach this book at once and keep it safely — it is your only means of buying clothing.

HOLD PAGES I–VII IN ONE HAND AND

TEAR ALONG THIS LINE

Holder's National Registration No.

AoeK / 67 /

War work

Men and women working in factories were as important as soldiers. Factories made tanks, guns, trucks, ships, and planes. Workers made all kinds of war equipment – helmets, army boots, blankets, uniforms, parachutes, radios. Many factories kept working night and day. Even when a factory was hit by bombs, it was often working again in a few days.

People worked hard. In 1940, workers in aircraft factories worked up to 70 hours a week, which is about twice as long as most people work today. Many women worked alongside men, doing the same jobs. From 1941, all women aged 20 to 30 had to do war work. For many, this meant leaving home for the first time, to go to another town. Thousands of Scots moved south to work in English factories. Women took over many jobs usually done by men who were away in the **armed forces**. They drove buses, repaired trucks, and flew planes from factories to airfields.

▼ This photo shows women of the Auxiliary Territorial Service repairing an RAF *Hurricane* fighter plane.

People from all over the Commonwealth came to Britain to help. For example, by 1943 more than 2,000 volunteers from the West Indies had come to Britain.

Advertising posters were used to boost the war effort. "Come into the factories" urged one poster. Another poster showed British workers wasting time, while Germans worked non-stop. The message was: "Your opposite number works fast. You must beat him".

Women in work

- By 1943, 90 per cent of single women in Britain were doing war work.
- In 1943, 80 per cent of married women were also doing war work.
- By 1944, a third of the workers in Britain's engineering factories were women.
- By 1945, more than 80,000 women were doing farm work, as "land girls".

▼ This double bar graph shows how many planes were built by countries at war in 1939 and 1944. Do you think this affected the outcome of the war?

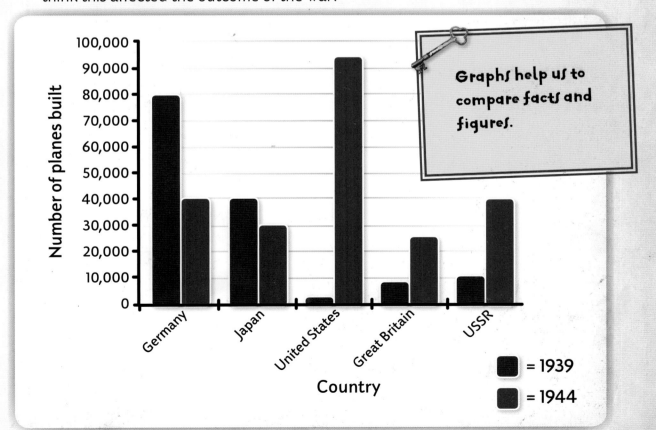

Graphs help us to compare facts and figures.

= 1939
= 1944

Rationing

Food **rationing** began in 1940. Each person was given a ration book. The government fixed the ration – how much of the most important foods, such as milk, butter, meat, and eggs, a person could have each week. Children got roughly half as much as adults. Rationing made sure everyone got a fair share.

In wartime Britain, people did most of their shopping in local shops, where the shopkeeper usually knew them. The shopkeeper checked people's ration books before serving them. Clothes, paper, petrol, and soap (the soap ration was one bar a month) were also rationed.

Since eggs were rationed, people tried dried egg powder. Mixed with water, it made quite good scrambled eggs. Chocolate and ice cream became rare treats, and there were no bananas. Why? Bananas came in ships from the sunny Caribbean and other warm places. Now every ship was needed to carry guns, tanks, or soldiers. People could still eat apples, pears, and other fruit grown in Britain.

Wartime cookery books showed people how to cook vegetables in new ways, to make up for the rationing of meat and other foods. ▶

VEGETABLES for VICTORY

Ambrose Heath

Ration books and wartime recipes show us what food people ate during the war.

▲ These children are being shown how to look after a vegetable garden during the school summer holiday in 1940.

Many people grew vegetables, as part of a "Dig for Victory" campaign. Children planted school gardens. Potatoes and carrots were plentiful, so people were told to eat more of them. People were often hungry, but surprisingly many became healthier than they were before the war.

A typical wartime menu

Breakfast
- National Wholemeal Loaf toast, with margarine (cereals were rationed)
- glass of milk (if there was any), or a cup of tea, with no sugar

Lunch
- carrot soup and a Spam sandwich
- apple and a slice of cake made with dried egg
- Carrolade drink (carrot and swede juice)

Dinner
- woolton pie (potatoes and other vegetables in pastry)
- portman pudding (steamed pudding made with flour, fat, carrot, potato, raisins, and a little sugar)

Make do and mend

Many ships carrying food, oil, and other materials faced attacks from enemy submarines. Many ships were lost at sea. This meant there was a shortage not just of some foods, such as wheat for making bread, but also of paper, clothing materials, and metals.

To make up for this, everyone tried to **recycle** waste paper, old pots and pans, and even dinner leftovers. To save fuel, people were told to walk instead of using buses. They burned less coal on fires and turned out lights. Park railings were sawn off and melted down. Children went around the streets to collect scrap metal, hoping old saucepans would soon turn into a new *Spitfire* fighter plane!

Clothes were **rationed**, so people tried to "make do and mend". This meant making clothes or reusing old clothes. Leaflets showed "Mrs Sew and Sew" giving tips on how to knit scarves and woolly hats, and how to make a coat from a blanket. In 1942, people could buy "utility" clothes, designed to use less material and last longer. There was utility furniture, too.

Food scraps went into bins, and were taken to farms, where hungry pigs gobbled up the leftovers.

Wartime economy

In 1938, spending on clothes was about £20 a year for each person. In 1943, it was only £7 10s (£7.50). A "siren suit" (like a modern-day tracksuit with a hood) for children "to keep them warm and cosy in an emergency" cost about 75p. The average wage in 1943 was between £3 and £5 a week.

Statistics like this show how the war affected people's daily lives.

Fun fact

Nylon stockings were not often on sale in shops. So some women painted their legs with coloured dye, which made it look as if they were wearing stockings.

▲ This photo was part of a recycling campaign. It showed people in Hammersmith, London, handing over scrap metal and waste paper for salvage.

Wartime fun

Many toy factories switched to making war equipment, so new toys were hard to find. Children swapped old toys. Any new toys were usually made of paper or card. Rubber, plastics, wood, and metal were too valuable for toys.

▼ A toy factory, October 1939. New dolls are being put into uniforms ready for the first wartime Christmas.

War toys included model planes, toy tanks, and battleships to float in the bath. Books had exciting stories about brave children defeating enemy spies, and pictures to help spot an enemy plane. Card games and jigsaws were good for passing the time in the **shelter**. A version of the Happy Families card game had funny pictures of people **evacuees** might have met in the countryside.

There were still parties at Christmas and birthdays, and treats, such as going to the "pictures" (films). Millions of people visited cinemas each week. They usually watched two films, plus a cartoon and a **newsreel** of war news. At home, families listened to BBC radio, which broadcast news, talks, music, comedy shows, and children's programmes. Television had started in 1936, but programmes were stopped when war began.

Some things children did during the war

- Collected bits of crashed planes and bomb cases (shrapnel)
- Played on bombsites (even though told not to)
- Watched cowboy films at the cinema
- Tried chewing gum for the first time (from US troops)
- Threw darts at a picture of Hitler
- Tried the jive and jitterbug, the new dance crazes from the United States
- Dug in the "Victory Garden" or at home
- Read the latest *Just William* book
- Listened to *Children's Hour* on the radio
- Made sure the **blackout** curtains were drawn
- Wrote letters to dad in the army or sister away doing war work
- Listened to music on a wind-up gramophone, which was a machine for playing records.

▲ Christmas in the shelter, 1940. This family celebrated early, on 23 December, because father would be working on Christmas Day.

Children did some ordinary things, and some unusual wartime things.

27

Future plans

In May 1944, Joan Dingwall, a young woman working in Sussex, was on a bus to Eastbourne. She was surprised to see "every field and farmyard crammed with military equipment – tanks, guns, the lot …"

What she saw was preparation for what is known as D-Day – the **Allies' invasion** of France on 6 June 1944. By May 1945, Germany was defeated, and in September 1945, Japan also surrendered. People celebrated peace with street parties, parades, and church services.

Much rebuilding was now needed. After six years of war, cities were in ruins and millions of people were homeless.

Millions of people died in World War II. To prevent any more such terrible wars, the United Nations Organization was set up to help keep peace around the world. There have been wars since 1945, but no world war.

▲ This photo shows a street party, one of thousands held to celebrate VE (Victory in Europe) Day on 8 May 1945.

World War II deaths

This table shows the estimated number of people killed during the war, and how many of them were in the **armed forces** or were **civilians**.

	Armed forces deaths	Civilian deaths
Allies	13,750,000	15,250,000
Axis Powers	5,650,000	2,100,000
Total	19,400,000	17,350,000

Timeline

1938   **Gas masks** are given to people in Britain in case of **air raids**; Germany takes over Austria

1939
August   **Evacuation** begins in Britain
1 September   Germany **invades** Poland
3 September   Britain and France go to war with Germany

1940
January   Food **rationing** begins in Britain
August   Battle of Britain is at its peak
September   The **Blitz** begins

1941
22 June   German armies invade USSR (Russia)
7 December   Japanese planes attack United States naval base of Pearl Harbor, Hawaii
8 December   United States and Britain declare war on Japan

1943
January   The **Allies** begin bombing Germany from airfields in Britain
September   Allied armies invade Italy

1944
6 June   D-Day, Allied armies land in Normandy in France to begin the freeing of German-occupied Western Europe

1945
March   Allied armies invade Germany
30 April   Russian armies enter Berlin; Germany's leader Adolf Hitler kills himself
7 May   Germany surrenders
8 May   VE (Victory in Europe) Day
6/9 August   The Allies drop atomic bombs on Japanese cities of Hiroshima and Nagasaki
2nd September   Official date of Japan's surrender; World War II is over

Glossary

air raid attack on a target by aircraft dropping bombs

Allies Britain, France, United States, USSR, and other nations that fought against the Axis powers

armed forces army, navy, and air force

Axis Powers Germany, Japan, Italy, and nations that fought against the Allies

blackout measures to reduce all lights at night, to hide possible targets from the enemy

Blitz short for *blitzkrieg*, German for "lightning war"; used to describe the German bombing of Britain that began in 1940

casualty person injured or killed during a war

civil defence arrangements to protect towns and cities from enemy attack, especially from the air

civilian person who is not in the armed forces

evacuation movement from danger to a safer place. In World War II, children were evacuated from towns to the countryside.

evacuee person who has been evacuated

evidence picture, writing, object, or someone's account, that tells us what things were like at a particular time

gas mask rubber face mask to protect the wearer from breathing in poison gas

invasion attack by one country on another, by sending armies onto its land

Nazi member of the National Socialist German Workers party, led by Adolf Hitler

newsreel programme of news films shown at the cinema

rationing government control of the sale of food, fuel, clothes, and other goods

recycling cutting down on waste by using materials again

shelter place to go to for protection in an air raid, usually underground, but also indoors

Find out more

Books

Usborne Britsh History: The Second World War, Henry Brook,
 Rob Lloyd Jones, and Conrad Mason (Usborne Publishing Ltd, 2008)
The World at War: World War II (series), Brian Williams (Heinemann
 Library, 2005)

Websites

Look inside a wartime house, take a virtual shopping trip with your ration
book, and much more on this website:
www.bbc.co.uk/history/ww2children

Find out lots of information about London during World War II:
www.lgfl.net/lgfl/accounts/holnet/upload/learningzone/
 londonatwar/index.html

Explore wartime documents, objects, and people's memories of the Blitz:
www.museumoflondon.org.uk/archive/exhibits/blitz/index.html

Places to visit

Imperial War Museum
Lambeth Road, London SE1 6HZ

Imperial War Museum North
The Quays, Trafford Wharf
Manchester M17 1TZ

National War Museum
Edinburgh Castle
Edinburgh EH1 2NG

D-Day Museum
Clarence Esplanade
Southsea PO5 3NT

Index